The Lodge Almoner

The Lodge Almoner

Charles J Carter

LEWIS MASONIC
Books

Other titles by the same author
   The Director of Ceremonies
   The Lodge Secretary
   The Inner Guard and Deacons

© 1992
Charles J Carter

First published in England 1992
by Lewis Masonic, Ian Allan Regalia Ltd
Coombelands House, Coombelands Lane
Addlestone, Surrey, KT15 1HY

ISBN 0 85318 195 0

British Library Cataloguing-in-Publication Data.
A catalogue record for this book is available from
the British Library.

Printed in Great Britain by
Latimer Trend & Company Ltd, Plymouth, Devon

Contents

About The Author

Charles James Carter was initiated into the Three Pillars Lodge No 4923 in May 1962, became Master in 1971 and Secretary the following year. In 1971 he became Founding Secretary of the Plantagenets Lodge No 8409 in the Province of Kent and Master in 1973. He served the office of Preceptor and Director of Ceremonies for ten years.

In 1977 he was promoted to Provincial Deputy Grand Director of Ceremonies a rank he was to hold for ten years before being promoted to Assistant Provincial Grand Master (West Kent) in 1987.

He was appointed to the rank of Past Assistant Grand Director of Ceremonies in the craft in 1981 and promoted to Past Senior Grand Deacon in 1988. In the Royal Arch he was appointed to the rank of Past Grand Standard Bearer in 1985.

He is the current Chief Executive and Secretary of the Quatuor Coronati Correspondence Circle, a post he has held since 1984, where he is responsible for the world wide operations of the well known Correspondence Circle of Quatuor Coronati Lodge to which he was elected a full member in May 1992.

He is an Honorary member of thirty eight lodges and fifteen chapters both in the United Kingdom and Overseas.

Chapter 1:

The Overall Role

When first viewed through the eyes of the inexperienced or newer member of a lodge the role of the Almoner can perhaps appear sometimes to be a sinecure. An elderly Past Master usually with a smiling cheerful countenance, is conducted to the East and invested with a collar which he has on many occasions worn for years. A few muttered words of thanks for his past services by the Master of the lodge then ensue and he returns to his seat. For the rest of the year he carries on to a greater or lesser extent, with his traditional role of caring for the membership and their dependants.

No matter what situation he encounters throughout the coming year, out of sight of the members of the lodge for the most part he is expected to cope with every eventuality which comes his way and very frequently he does so without recognition or acknowledgement of the work he performs. Frequently the brother so appointed to this role brings with him years of knowledge and first hand experience. This knowledge may well have been accumulated through some form of working environment which has equipped him with this specialization which fortunately he has subsequently been able to use to the advantage of his brethren and their dependants.

The role of the Almoner has in recent times been recognized and acknowledged by Grand Lodge to have a greater degree of importance than perhaps had previously been the case. Taken with the greater longevity of the population as a whole together with the obvious effects this has upon, not only the membership of the lodge itself but also the dependants of those same members, the work of the Almoner in the future is going to grow and of that he may be certain. In his traditional role the lodge Almoner has a duty to advise, assist and where necessary seek out the help and assistance of the various masonic and outside bodies for both possible financial help, housebound assistance and sometimes permanent residential care.

The actual role of the lodge Almoner is therefore somewhat different from that first perceived by a newly made brother of what the office encompasses simply because the greater part of the work undertaken by the brother so appointed takes place out of sight of the members and much of it is very often not even known or reported to the lodge itself. Almoners tend by their very nature to be less than demonstrative of their efforts on behalf of the lodge and its members.

The purpose of this book therefore is to seek to help, assist, and perhaps most importantly, point in the right direction the newly appointed Almoner who finds himself quite suddenly and without warning in a situation with which he is totally unfamiliar and one with which he has not the remotest idea as to how he should start to deal with that problem, which organization he should approach first, or to whom he should turn for advice.

The reader will quickly note from the variety of the headings of the chapters of this book that the range of knowledge and caring situations into which the new Almoner can find himself plunged quite suddenly are many and varied. It will be a very experienced Almoner indeed who can, without reference, handle every situation with precisely the single or varied form of approach that the vagaries of the role present to him.

Unlike any other office in the lodge, with perhaps the single exception of the Secretary, the office of Almoner can be held by a brother for many years without presenting any particular difficulty and then quite suddenly a situation arises with which the Almoner is either totally unfamiliar or with which he is completely unprepared to deal. This book has been written for such occasions together with, it is hoped, a goodly amount of sound advice which if taken will assist all Almoners, both those of long standing as well as those who have recently been appointed.

It is hoped that the reader will benefit from reading the chapters contained in this book even if none of the situations outlined or referred to ever come his way. Remember it is better to have the information and not need it, than need it and not have it.

Chapter 2:

The Lodge Records of Members

It would seem to be obvious to anyone who thinks seriously about the subject that a first class set of membership records is essential not only for the Secretary but also for anyone who has a duty to care for or be concerned with the members of the lodge and their dependants. Such sensible planning however may not always be so obvious particularly to those who do not have reason to think seriously about such matters. This potential lack of foresight can be fraught with problems, particularly for the lodge Almoner, as when a situation suddenly occurs where such records are needed and are found to be wanting it is invariably the case that there is no one available to supply the information required. It can quickly be appreciated therefore that records collected at an early stage and kept fully up-to-date can, when the situation demands be of the utmost help to the responsible Almoner.

Good planning, adequate forward thinking and, especially amongst the elderly members of the lodge, an up-to-date note of the member's next of kin, are essential, particularly if the member is living on his own and perhaps has lost his partner some years earlier. In such a circumstance the lodge Almoner may find himself undertaking a much bigger role than he might at first have thought possible, hence the essential requirement of good lodge records.

Let us start at the beginning. When a man applies for membership of the Craft and in due time completes an application form with all its required information that is the basis on which to begin the compilation of the information of that potential brother's personal file. After the applicant's form has been read and has been balloted for at the next meeting and the candidate has subsequently been initiated, it is always advisable to arrange a short meeting with him quite privately and away from the lodge meetings or the lodge of instruction and for that matter all other masonic occasions, for the

3

things you have to discuss with him require the right atmosphere, plenty of time and the correct ambiance if a mutually relaxed and beneficial conversation is to ensue.

What then are those things the Almoner should discuss with a newly made brother so early in his membership? We already know where he lives, whether he is married and what his profession or occupation is stated to be. We also know his age and his proposer and seconder into the Craft so what more could we possibly wish to know and perhaps more than that, have the right to ask? The answer is that we do not start with a series of questions but rather with a conversation piece about his future membership and the part that the lodge will play in ensuring that he both enjoys and benefits from the association he will have with the Craft in general and the fellow members of his mother lodge in particular.

We could start by ascertaining what he knows about the masonic charities and if the answers given show a complete lack of knowledge on the subject, make a mental note to ask the Charity Steward to talk to him at some stage in the future. Such lack of information can however give the opportunity to mention the basic outline of those things which are considered to be very dear to our membership of the Craft.

A few words on the Masonic Trust for Girls and Boys, its various operations and facilities, particularly if he has a young family which can often be the case, will ensure that a two-way conversation can be held. Mention of the school at Rickmansworth and the opportunities for assistance in the case of need will allow a useful discourse to be held. Encourage questions at every stage.

The Royal Masonic Benevolent Institution and its many homes for the elderly can also be explained in detail and this should give the new member an opportunity to ask questions about the range of facilities available. From your point of view as the Almoner, you can say that the lodge requires you as its Almoner to keep a full and up-to-date record card for every member and that you would appreciate his co-operation in ensuring that the lodge has as complete a record as possible in case it has to assist him or his family at short notice.

You of course must decide what you feel it is necessary to ask but such simple things as the name of the member's wife and those of his children, their ages, his next of kin, and similar personal details can be asked and answered without any embarrassment on his or your part if dealt with in a relaxed conversational style and by asking in a positive manner.

Details collected at this stage of a member's masonic career could well be of benefit when perhaps he is no longer there to ask and you may well find yourself dealing with a bereaved widow and children. Above all what you will achieve from such a meeting will be the instilling into the newly made brother the awareness that Free-masonry is much more than an organization conducting strange ceremonies but is a charitable brotherhood which takes its members future care very seriously no matter how junior they might be. This first meeting could well be the best grounding that the newly made mason will ever get and which could well fashion his attitude towards the Craft for the rest of his masonic career. Do not fail to emphasize that all this is being done in a desire to be helpful and that it is not a question of prying into his private affairs.

This is a facet of your role, brother Almoner, which you may not have considered but one which you can now perhaps appreciate is vitally important even to those who are unlikely to need your services at this precise moment.

Chapter 3:

The Member's Doctor and Next of Kin

It may surprise you to see the heading of this chapter so near to the front of the book but upon reflection it is obvious why such a vital piece of information is an essential ingredient in the information package about the new member. It is probably not within the experience of the average lodge Almoner to know or appreciate the difficulties that can occur when the name, address and telephone number of the doctor of an ailing member is unknown and is required urgently particularly if reference has to be made to that member's medical records. Asking a newly made member for such details is quite easy and makes the task of updating future information a simple matter particularly when he changes his abode as will invariably happen during his years of membership within the lodge. There is also a valuable side feature of this action, which is to demonstrate in a meaningful way to the newly initiated brother just how much Freemasons care for each other.

Whilst Brother Almoner might well imagine that such information is likely to be required only for the older and perhaps single members whose expectation of requiring medical assistance will by the very nature of passing time be greater than that of the younger member, it would be quite wrong to leave the obtaining of such information until he clearly becomes a sick man. Worse still, until the time comes when preparation must be made; you had better be prepared for his indeterminate demise or at the very least, his now obviously few closing years. Obtaining this information when the new member joins the lodge will take no longer than obtaining the same information 25 years later but the advantage to be gained is that you have such an important fact recorded for that perhaps never needed occasion but available nevertheless just in case it does arise.

If you need proof of the 'being prepared' syndrome, remember there are many things which most of us do in our lives with just this idea in mind. House and personal insurance and medical insurance are some examples. We have awaiting our possible need such facilities as fire engines, ambulances and hospitals and we all know what we have to do to bring them into immediate use should the occasion demand. Why then should we treat the new member with any less care and consideration than we would wish to be treated ourselves?

Detailing the member's next of kin should prove somewhat easier albeit it is essential that an up-to-date situation is maintained, for brethren do lose their partners and thus the records of such information will require updating from time to time.

Chapter 4:

The Widows of Past Members and Other Dependants

The requirement to write this chapter might perhaps appear unnecessary for it will be obvious to even the most recently appointed Almoner that the ongoing care and happiness of a deceased member's partner will form a permanent role to be encompassed in his overall brief. It is perhaps best to try to divide this particular facet of the Almoner's role into two.

In the first case the Almoner will be dealing with the known widow of a member whom he has met many times perhaps at ladies' nights and other social functions and is therefore able to make a direct approach. He may well know the family circumstances and the immediate circle of children or other relatives who are available to assist the newly widowed wife with the many new responsibilities with which she finds herself coping for the first time in her life. In other words the job of ensuring her on-going care is perhaps fully done and nothing requires to be managed in that direction other than ensuring that her future monetary situation is such that she can manage to meet her financial obligations without a severe reduction in her standard of living. Do remember to read the section on Annuities from the RMBI if it should be found necessary to assist a widow for the reasons outlined.

Let us now turn to the second case which is where brother Almoner, upon taking over the role, finds that he has perhaps inherited one or two cases which concern the care of widows of members who died long before he himself became a member of the lodge. This situation frequently exists, perhaps more often than might be imagined. There are also cases of brethren dying who have been members of the lodge for many years but perhaps due to distance or old age have not been seen in the lodge for perhaps ten, fifteen, twenty years or even more and whose faces are now less than familiar to the majority of the membership. What of these members? They are after all just as entitled to our care and concern as a brother whom we have had face to face dealings over many years, are they not? We shall assume for the sake of the newly appointed Almoner that he has no real records on which to rely for historical facts and is forced to start from scratch. Clearly he may well be dealing with a lady of advanced years whose ability to recall or remember may be far from pristine. Obviously at this point he may well have to consider a personal visit to the lady concerned. This should always be preceded by a telephone call or letter making a clear appointment during which he should suggest that if there are any family members who would care to be present he would welcome the opportunity of talking to them. Let us assume that the meeting has been arranged and the polite introductions have been completed, what then should ensue? It is accepted that the brother appointed to this office in the lodge will in all probability not have had any formal training for the role so that the following suggestions may perhaps be of assistance.

Clearly brother Almoner should explain that his role on behalf of the lodge, is to ensure that the widow and dependant relatives of the late member are financially secure and that they have no immediate problems with which they are unable to cope. The question of the longer term financial requirements for those same dependants is an entirely different subject and will require a much longer and more detailed discussion, perhaps even with the aid of outside sources and advisers, should this prove necessary. The manner in which brother Almoner puts his questions to the bereaved spouse will need extremely careful handling but by a series of gentle questions and the skilful development of the answers he receives into other questions, he should be able to extract the facts he requires from the person with whom he is dealing. It must be remembered that many ladies have for most of their married lives relied upon their husbands to manage their joint financial affairs and have little idea at all of managing savings, bank accounts and less still if such investments as stocks and shares are involved. Brother Almoner may himself need to take advice from a competent source if his own knowledge does not extend to this area of experience. It is very risky to give financial guidance unless one is qualified in such matters. Families will usually deal with most of the immediate personal financial matters but here we are dealing with a situation of a lady left completely alone and perhaps in her late eighties or nineties.

It is virtually certain that every case will require to be handled in a different manner from any other. It is also to be recommended that a period of at least two to three weeks after the funeral be allowed to elapse before such a meeting is scheduled, albeit an earlier contact should be made to ensure that the person concerned knows that help is immediately at hand if required.

Finally it must be remembered that the dependants of members who have been excluded or resigned are equally entitled to our care and consideration. Just because a brother has been excluded or has resigned his membership, that is no reason for his dependants to be deprived of our care and protection of their future needs or requirements. This fact is often not appreciated by Almoners but it is nevertheless an essential ingredient in the overall knowledge of an efficient Almoner.

Chapter 5:

The Role of the RMBI

The Royal Masonic Benevolent Institution based at 20, Great Queen Street, London, WC2B 5BG. (Tel No: 071-405 8341) is the prime masonic entity concerned with providing residential accommodation and annuities for the elderly. The RMBI also provides loans for the improvement of houses, and operates a welfare visiting scheme.

The role of the RMBI is much wider in fact than the average lodge Almoner might imagine. The following list of dependants are all eligible for consideration provided always that their circumstances warrant such consideration: widows, dependant children, spinster daughters, spinster sisters, also dependant mothers of deceased Freemasons who must be of at least 60 years of age, but younger if incapacitated. There are certain qualifying factors involved which, in the case of a member of the Craft, are that he shall have been a subscribing member of an English Constitution lodge for at least 15 years. In the case of a dependant of a member of the craft, a period of ten years applies. It is always advisable to ask the Secretary of the Institution for the full details relevant to assistance being provided either residential or by way of an annuity.

There is very close co-operation between the RMBI and the Grand Charity which operates from Freemasons' Hall, London, (Tel No: 071-831 9811 ext 239) in all matters concerning annuities which in the majority of cases are provided by the Grand Charity (see chapter six). In London, lodge Almoners should apply directly to the RMBI Welfare department at 110 Main Road, Sidcup, Kent DA14 6NG (081-302 6225), for residential consideration and to the Grand Charity or the RMBI for all matters connected with financial help either by annuity or a one off payment to cover a particular need. In the Provinces and Districts all such applications should be directed through the appropriate Provincial or District Grand Secretary. The RMBI also provides holidays for annuitants, especially directed towards those who might otherwise not be able to afford such a break.

Both the Grand Charity and the RMBI have a wide range of facilities available to members of the Craft and their dependants and the wise lodge Almoner will make it an urgent part of his information gathering immediately after appointment to acquaint himself with such information, so that if and when the need arises he will not be found incompetent and unable to advise. Such a crisis is most decidedly not the time to start learning his role.

It would be unwise in such a generalized book as this to try to encompass every facility available to members of the Craft and their dependants. Lodge Almoners are therefore earnestly advised to ensure that they know whom to contact if and when a situation requiring the help of either the RMBI or the Grand Charity arises.

Finally it should always be remembered that officials of both the aforementioned institutions are experts in the day to day care of the elderly and infirm and that they have an intimate knowledge of the most current legislation available. The advice of either institution should be sought as soon as possible when a problem arises in an area in which you are either not experienced at all or where your present knowledge is perhaps less than up to date.

Chapter 6:

Annuities for Needy Brethren and their Dependants

An RMBI annuity is a regular amount of money paid four times a year to a brother or his dependant or dependants. Such payments as are made are related to the individual's total income from pensions and interest on savings. The criteria which is applied to the granting of such annuities varies from time to time and brother Almoner is recommended to seek advice should this requirement fall within his orbit of operation. There is a legal government limit on the amount of an annuity payable before it becomes a taxable sum or other pensions are reduced.

The agreement to pay and the payment itself do not take place until after the submission of the appropriate forms which can be obtained from either the RMBI or the Grand Charity, both of whose telephone numbers are given in the previous chapter. It is normal for an interview by a Welfare Visitor to take place (usually in the petitioners own home) before a grant is made. Once a person becomes an annuitant a permanent file is opened by the RMBI or Grand Charity and brother Almoner should ensure that this file is kept up to date by advising these charities of any changes in the annuitants circumstances. Both of these institutions work very closely together to ensure that maximum care and attention is given to elderly or infirm annuitants.

Where the lodge Almoner suspects financial worries he should investigate with great care the overall income of a dependant and if his findings are such that an annuity is called for then an application should be made without delay.

The RMBI has a home at Hove in Sussex exclusively available for annuitants who prefer or require to be within an environment whereby their care is supervised and their own involvement with the day to day requirement to provide food, electricity and gas are taken care of by the home itself.

Finally remember that when dependants are discussing such financial matters with a 'stranger' for that after all is what brother Almoner is, the question of pride will frequently present itself to the enquirer. It will take skill and aptitude if this facet of his duties is to be accomplished without conveying the appearance of intrusion into private matters. In this respect it is perhaps helpful to talk about the departed brother's support of the charities and his knowledge that those same charities would be readily available for his dependants in the event of their being needed after his departure and that he would have been disappointed to think that such help had been refused.

Remember that it's not what you say it is the manner in which you say it that counts.

Chapter 7:

Members of London Lodges

Where financial difficulties are encountered by the spouse or dependant of a member or by the member himself who is or was a member of a London lodge of at least the rank of Master Mason there exists a special fund called the London Grand Rank Fund, the purpose of which is to assist in such circumstances and this is governed by Rule 61 of the *Book of Constitutions*. This fund is for the use of members and their dependants, the details of which are shown in the *Book of Constitutions*. This fund was established in 1909 to provide for London Masons the additional financial assistance provided in other Provinces and Districts by their respective Benevolent Funds.

If brother Almoner is appointed by a London lodge it is recommended that he talks to the London Grand Rank Association whose many services are readily available to any brother who has been, or is, a member of a London lodge. The LGRA visiting brother scheme is of particular merit where a brother or dependant is resident some distance from London. Petitions are usually considered on the Monday before the meetings of the Petitions Committee of the Council of The Grand Charity. Detailed information can be obtained from the LGRA office in Freemasons' Hall (Tel No: 071-405 1671) and also the Grand Charity (Tel No: 071-831 9811).

Fees of honour for appointment to London Grand Rank and London Grand Chapter Rank form the basis of new income to the fund and these together with its investment income provide the monies available for meeting such requests for assistance as may arise from time to time.

Chapter 8:

The Royal Masonic Hospital

This well known Masonic Institution has its roots in an original fund started in 1911. It has occupied various premises since 1914, the present building at Ravenscourt Park in west London having been opened in 1933. The Royal Masonic Hospital is an independent hospital for acute general medicine and surgery cases. It also offers extensive medical check-up facilities on a fee paying basis. The hospital exists primarily to provide medical facilities for Freemasons and their dependants and, although realistic fees are charged, it is the proud claim of the hospital that treatment to a Freemason has never been refused because he could not pay.

Although not a casualty hospital it will admit patients in an emergency at any time. Admissions to the hospital may be achieved by the following methods:

Emergency Admissions:
are arranged at any time by telephoning the duty registrar. This should be done by the doctor attending the patient.

Urgent Admissions:
within 72 hours arranged between the patient's doctor and Patients' Services Department.

Non-Urgent Admissions:
the patient's doctor should complete one of the Hospital's medical report forms.

16

IT IS NOT NECESSARY TO CONTACT THE LODGE BEFORE ADMISSION
Facilities exist for out-patient treatment.

The telephone number of the Hospital is 071–748 4611

Brother Almoner is advised to read the chapter headed 'The New Masonic Samaritan Fund' which deals with financial assistance for those who cannot meet the full costs of the charges incurred or indicated.

Chapter 9:

Getting the Elderly Member to a Meeting

There can scarcely be a sadder reply to the question "why don't we see you any more at our meetings?" than that rendered by a housebound or elderly brother, "I would willingly come if only I could get some help with transport." Care after an illness, injury or bereavement is of course admirable but a goodly contribution of forethought about the existing conditions of members and their apparent lessening of attendance or non-attendance over a period of time is also called for by the thinking Almoner.

It is a wise Almoner who notices the signs which indicate that a member is perhaps past his active years and now finds the effort of travelling to a meeting on his own more than he wishes to undertake. In doing this and taking some action on it he will be carrying out a very valuable service to his lodge and to the Master who appointed him. It is a relatively simple matter to find a brother who lives not far from the ailing member or one who could make a detour to collect and return a member particularly if the older member is virtually housebound or goes out very infrequently. Such a member will welcome and look forward to being transported from his own front door to the meeting and being returned later that evening.

Such a kind action brings forth many benefits. Firstly, it shows to the members of the lodge and their guests that the lodge cares about ALL its members. Secondly, it shows to the member thus cared for that his membership, although not as active these days as it used to be, is still considered valuable to the lodge and that he is a treasured asset which the lodge wishes to retain. Thirdly, that member will spend many happy hours thinking about the meeting before the day itself arrives and a similar period of reflection after the meeting is over.

It should always be remembered that loneliness is probably the emotion that is most feared by the elderly and housebound and the opportunity to get out, albeit for a few hours at a time, means so much and the effort thus expended in organizing this kind action is more than repaid by the gratitude of the member. What is more, surely this is an example of Freemasonry in action—is it not?

Chapter 10:

Hospital Visiting

We now live in a world where statistically we are told we should each expect to be hospitalized at least three times in our lives. Clearly a number of members will pay short visits to hospitals lasting just a few days and it is not this type of hospitalization that is referred to here. We are considering the member who for many reasons is hospitalized for many weeks, months or possibly permanently with a terminal illness.

Many members of the lodge will, upon receiving notice of a brother's incarceration, wish to visit him and make sure that he is kept cheerful and has a steady stream of visitors to whom to relate from his interests outside the hospital. All too frequently in this situation one of the following can occur. Firstly, there will be an un-organized retinue of visitors from the lodge as well as the member's own family and friends. This can lead to many problems not least of which is tiring the member at a time when he should be resting or recuperating, perhaps from an operation. Secondly, there may well be a wish on the part of the immediate relatives for privacy for the member of their family, especially if the illness is of a slowly deteriorating type or has been stated to be terminal.

In either of the aforementioned cases it is beneficial to remember that there is a strain upon the family related to regular hospital visiting, especially when it takes place every day and sometimes perhaps twice a day. Individuals frequently find it difficult to provide enough new conversation to fill an hour of time each and every day and the strain of being cheerful and projecting that cheerfulness can tell upon the most skilful and well meaning partner or relative. Experience has shown that if a lodge Almoner discusses the question of visiting with the nearest relative he can usually obtain an agreement to be allocated, say two visiting periods a week on a permanent basis. This system does two things, firstly it relieves the family of the responsibility of visiting for two evenings a week and enables them to do something other than go to the hospital. Secondly it means that the Almoner can build a rota of different brethren so that the hospitalized member sees a new face at each allocated visiting period. Conversations from different people from a variety of backgrounds can have a lifting effect on the spirits of a patient and keep him in touch with the outside world.

Once the Almoner has gained this agreement he can then, by telephoning the members of the lodge, compile a list on the basis of filling in the names of brethren willing to visit against designated dates and times. Once this has been achieved, say for two or three weeks in advance, then a new list can be compiled and by so doing the patient is shown that his brethren do care about his well being and the family are shown that the patient's lodge members whilst caring for him, do not wish to interfere in the programme scheduled by the family but wish to act as a relief to that schedule by giving additional help to them in their time of need.

What is absolutely imperative is that when a member of the lodge agrees to visit a patient in hospital, he should make quite certain that he does so and at the time agreed. Nothing is more soul-destroying than to wait in bed for a visitor who does not arrive or else arrives five minutes before the end of the visiting period. It is always wise not to dwell upon the illness of the patient but relate to the world outside and particularly those things which the patient will wish to participate in once again when he leaves the hospital.

Brother Almoner has of course a duty to make such reports of the progress or otherwise of the brethren of the lodge at all its meetings and he should remember to be extremely accurate in his reporting of the 'facts', and not his 'opinions' of what the future may hold for the sick brother. Forcasting the future is NOT part of his duty as Almoner of the lodge.

Chapter 11:

Telephone and their Practical Use

We live in a world where communication becomes faster and easier every single day. Dialling to Australia and America is as easy as dialling to the house next door and yet we frequently come across a situation where with a little thought the life of a once active and dedicated brother can be enhanced by a little thought and planning. Loneliness has already been mentioned as being the single biggest concern to brethren who are housebound and live their lives in comparative seclusion. Let us see what can be done to brighten that life and bring into it a little of the caring and compassion which are the watchwords of our order.

A brother who is able to receive telephone calls can be assisted to enjoy his lonely existence by a series of regular calls not just from the Almoner but a wide variety of the brethren within the lodge. It breaks up a boring evening to receive a cheerful call full of news of fellow brethren and their lives. A roster of ten brethren can make the difference between being forgotten and being tangibly remembered. One telephone call every five weeks or so from ten brethren will ensure that twice a week the housebound brother will know that he is not forgotten and that his brethren care about his wellbeing. It is surely not a difficult task for a caring lodge to set up and maintain a roster of brethren willing to undertake this simple but meaningful example of masonic brotherhood?

This system when established can be effectively promoted by getting housebound members to talk to each other at times of the day when telephone charges are at their lowest.

Remember and remember well, that the brother for whom you care today could so easily be you in five, ten, twenty or thirty years time. It's a sobering thought is it not?

Chapter 12:

Regular Visits to Elderly Members

In a perfect world where everything that can be done is done and everyone who is in need of care receives it, there would be little requirement for this chapter to be written. Sadly it is often the case that a member of a lodge once having been out of sight for a few years starts to become a distant memory in the minds of many of the brethren. His contemporaries remember him but they too are very probably getting on in years and have ageing problems similar to those of the brother who no longer attends. He is not known to the newer members and as the years pass fewer and fewer brethren remember the one who was once a most active participant in the affairs of the lodge and probably very much the life and soul of every meeting much as the newer members are today.

Our non-attending member probably continues to pay his subscription to the lodge and he receives his summonses on a regular basis but many of the new names appearing have little relevance to him for they are the 'faceless' new boys whom he has never met and is unlikely ever to meet. What a very sad scenario all this is to be sure and amazingly enough it need not happen, for with a little thought and action on the part of the active members, the older member who can no longer attend the meetings can so easily be kept in touch with events as they occur and made to feel part of the lodge which for so many years he had been an active member. How then do we achieve this 'utopian' dream?

Brother Almoner can ensure that the housebound member receives regular visits from some of the brethren of the lodge by constructing a similar roster to that recommended for hospital visiting, albeit not so often. A brother being visited once every month to six weeks looks forward to the visit and remembers afterwards the happy evening which he had talking over the events of yesteryear with brethren who knew, remembered and understood those happy

23

times. It is always a good idea for brother Almoner to take along on such visits one of the newer members of the lodge so that the older man can tell the younger member of events which he remembers connected with the lodge in the years in which he was an active member.

This serves two useful purposes, firstly it brings into the circle thus constructed a new face and one to which the housebound brother can relate should brother Almoner at some time not be able to manage his regular visit. Secondly, at the same time, the younger member is being trained in two valuable facets of his membership of the Craft which are those of compassion to the elderly and the relationship between the past and the present. You are by example training a potential Almoner of the future who may learn by this practical lesson just how much our brethren care for each other. Such visits when properly organized are worth so much both to the giver as well as the receiver. Try it and you will be surprised.

Where a brother in the circumstances described earlier is living at a distance which makes the aforementioned suggestion quite impractical, remember that the London Grand Rank Association operates a 'Visiting Brother Scheme' which can be activated by contacting the office of the LGRA at Freemasons' Hall, Great Queen Street, London. Arrangements will be made immediately for a visit to be made and for a report to be produced on the health and general condition of the brother concerned together with his immediate requirements if any. This facility is an excellent way of maintaining contact when long distances separate brother Almoner from the brethren for whom he is caring.

Chapter 13:

Loneliness is the Greatest Burden

There can surely be nothing to equal the suffering caused by loneliness. The writer well remembers his first experience of this form of
mental cruelty when he discussed with an elderly brother how he
spent his time in retirement and received the reply "Oh, looking
forward to the milkman coming every other day because it does give
me someone to talk to if only for a few minutes, otherwise my front
door never opens and I don't speak to a soul from one day to the
next." Can you begin to imagine what went through the mind of
that brother day after day as, without human contact, he faced yet
another day on his own with perhaps only the voices on the radio or
television for company?

This conversation was held with a brother whose working life in
the world of newspapers had been hectic, with deadlines to be met
and handling the constant updating of stories and more important
still, having a close constant working relationship with 'people'. Now
he had none, for those years of work were long past and his working
contemporaries, many of whom used to visit him during his early
retirement, are themselves either dead or very elderly. Brother
Almoner has a duty, yes a duty, to ensure that elderly members have
some form of contact with the outside world on a regular basis. This
can take many forms from visits by a wide range of people to telephone calls or letters and perhaps by taking him to a meeting. All of
these things break up a week and give the lonely brother something
to look forward to, and perhaps even more importantly, to think
about for days and weeks after the event.

We live today in a world where the speed of life is constantly
getting faster and faster and there appears little time for such mun-
dane things as popping in for the odd visit or making the occasional
telephone call, but these kindly acts mean so much to the lonely
member. Occasionally it is possible to find a member of another

lodge who lives very close to your own elderly member and a friendly ongoing relationship can be established between the two of them. This is to be encouraged for travelling time and distance can cause regular visits to be less frequent.

Thought should be given to alerting the social services if a brother is clearly seen to be coming to the point where his overall ability to care for himself has been reached. These services are in place within every council throughout the land and they have statutory obligations to care for the elderly. There are many ways in which such services can help and these are described in chapters 17 to 21.

Remember of course that the Royal Masonic Benevolent Institution has a welfare visitor service which can provide excellent assistance combined with up to date information on current legislation and allowances. Brother Almoner is recommended to use this facility for it exists to aid those who can no longer care completely for themselves. You should occasionally remind the brethren of your lodge that their donations and those of your lodge help this, our very own excellent organization, to provide such a service to our elderly members.

Chapter 14:

Care in the Community

We have already mentioned loneliness as being the single most dreaded facet of old age. The fact of being deprived of human contact on virtually a permanent basis is also known to be a major contributory factor to early death and, when combined with the natural ageing process, remove the zest for life so necessary for happiness and living a satisfactory existence.

Local councils are also aware of the importance of getting elderly people into both regular conversations and active participation with other similarly situated people in group activities. Many councils have day centres where the older member can enjoy a day out in an environment in which there is much to do if the person so attending wishes or alternatively the opportunity just to sit and talk if that is preferred. It is not at all unusual for caring councils to provide transport to and from such day centres for the less ambulant amongst those using these facilities. When a case exists where a brother is discovered living totally alone it is always advisable to enquire by telephone from the local council for the area in which the brother lives just which services are available. It might well be the case that there is some form of local activity meeting regularly near to the brother concerned in which he would be interested or something quite new in which he could be encouraged to participate.

It really is important both mentally as well physically for the brother concerned to get out of his abode and meet other people with whom he can converse and in addition participate in those things which held an interest for him in former years or perhaps in something with which he would now like to become involved.

You will also probably find that if the council concerned owns its own swimming baths, there is a regular weekly period set aside to enable the retired or elderly persons to use its facilities without the disturbance and noise associated with the younger and more boisterous members of society. Swimming provides an excellent means of toning up the majority of the muscles of the body and, as many physiotherapists will tell you, the action of swimming brings more of the bodies' muscles into play than any other exercise designed by man. If your charge is a swimmer, try to encourage him or her to participate, it really will help in more ways than one.

Some day care centres provide subsidized meals for elderly residents within their area of responsibility. Such meals are invariably well balanced protein wise and will help to ensure that the person taking such meals receives a goodly supply of the vitamins he or she requires to maintain good health. It is also very likely that the provision of such meals will contain many of the ingredients which individuals would not bother to prepare for themselves. This is just one of the benefits to be obtained from using such facilities where they exist. A full range of the facilities and services available can be obtained from most town halls or social services departments and brother Almoner is advised to get a full list each time he has a case in an area with which he is unfamilar. These services vary very considerably from council to council as well as from year to year so do not rely on the information you received five years ago to make a subjective judgement on what is or is not available. There will be many services with which you are not concerned but there may well be many more which you simply did not know existed, particularly for those with special needs.

Do enquire. A telephone call costs very little and can frequently assist you and your dependant brother or relative out of all proportion to the cost of the call. Local churches and chapels of all denominations also provide many services for the elderly and these also are well worth checking.

Chapter 15:

Christmas—that Special Time of Year

Christmas is surely the one time in the year when every Almoner shakes himself into action an ensures that the widows of previous members receive some form of communication be it Christmas cards, flowers, gift vouchers, chocolates or even a personal visit if the circumstances permit. Christmas after all is that special time of year when we tend to remember those whom we have not been able to visit or talk to for a long time and it gives us all the opportunity to correct that situation.

That a brother or his dependants should suffer with loneliness at Christmas is quite unforgivable. Although it does sometimes happen that a person wishes to be on their own and we must of course respect that wish, Christmas is nevertheess an opportunity to get the person out of their own environment for a few hours into an alternative venue with new people to meet and the chance to have fresh conversations and share a meal without having the necessity of cooking it. Many people simply do not wish to be seen receiving charity and it is the clever Almoner who can arrange such matters by allowing receivers to feel that it is they who are doing the giver a service by allowing him to feel helpful at this important time of the year.

The author knows of one Almoner who spends Christmas visiting those members under his care on Christmas day and Boxing day. With some of his charges on board he takes them for a car ride which may be the first time they have been outside their own door since the previous Christmas when he performed a similar exercise. There is much to be received from this form of action not only in gratitude but by seeing the happiness in the faces of those thus looked after. He has by such a simple act shown that most important facet of a caring Almoner namely that his charges are important to him and he has given of himself to care for them. Many variations of this theme can be investigated and tried to suit the requirements of the individuals concerned and brother Almoner should not be slow to involve his fellow brethren in the kindly acts he performs.

Important. Let it not be forgotten that just because you have been appointed the Almoner of and for the lodge, it does not mean that the rest of the lodge members are automatically relieved of their responsibility to assist in this important and valuable aspect of the lodge function. One lodge of the author's acquaintance carries out a rather nice exercise in ensuring that the children of a late brother's family receive cards and presents both at Christmas and also on their birthdays, an exercise they have carried out with conviction for over ten years now. What a wonderful introduction to Freemasonry in its finest form, that of a caring organization—it is in the formative years of a child's existence that many patterns for later life are cast.

Chapter 16:

Entitlements Under the NHS

The National Health Service, to which the majority of the population have contributed at some time or other to a greater or lesser degree has available a whole range of benefits and payments many of which are never claimed or used for the simple reason that the majority of those so entitled to them know nothing of their availability. Such benefits, be they cash, help in the home, or modifications to property to assist the elderly and infirm, are covered in a very wide variety of documents which are available from any DSS office. Since such benefits are altered, increased, modified or changed very regularly it would be unwise for a definitive listing to be given in a book such as this.

You may be quite sure that there are many many ways in which a housebound person can be helped to a better existence and certainly a better quality of life. Brother Almoner is urged therefore to make sure his knowledge on this subject is greater than it probably was on the day he was invested for the first time as the lodge Almoner. Councils have a wide variety of supplementary systems to augment those available from government schemes and since such additional benefits vary from council to council it would indeed be unwise to try to list those currently available. Do ask, for you will be quite surprised just what can be done without recourse to spending cash, either that of the lodge or of the brother or dependant. After all it is the right of the person so entitled to make a claim for these benefits, for after a lifetime of work and an equally long lifetime of making contributions to the funds of the NHS, the claimants or recipients of such benefits are surely only receiving that to which they are entitled— aren't they?

See also chapter 20 for details of help within the home in the form of grants for conversions and renovations.

Chapter 17:

The Social Services and What They Can Do To Help

We now enter a field of availability which once again will vary from council to council but in every case there is a statutory requirement for each council to provide minimal social care to the residents living within the confines of its authority.

Council social services will provide upon request and after satisfaction of need, a range of assisting supplements to help the housebound or infirm person. Such facilities can start with providing meals on wheels, to home helps, to modifying the home to ensure greater safety for the elderly, to providing a commode for a person who cannot climb stairs to visit the bathroom as well as a whole variety of other aids to assist comfort and safety within the home environment.

Brother Almoner needs to be the type of person who can deal with officialdom without a demanding attitude but with a firmness in reminding the officials concerned of their requirement to provide these services on a statutory basis. This does not mean and is not meant to suggest any form of 'telling them how to do their job' for such an approach will invariably work to the detriment of the person brother Almoner is trying to help. Using psychology in such an enquiring situation can and does bring forth without any difficulty, the assistance of the majority of officials and it is always a very nice approach to ask for such help rather than to demand it. At the same time it is always as well to know before you begin the task of asking the local council for help, just what those statutory requirements are, in case you meet some resistance and therefore find that you have to remind them gently that they have a duty to perform such a service 'by law'. Persuasion is always better than using the heavy hand but on occasions it does not do any harm to let the person to whom you are talking see that you have a copy of the government legislation covering care of the elderly and infirm in the home. If it does nothing else it will make them realize that you are a person who knows what he is talking about, and that surely can be no bad thing.

Finally remember that if the situation regarding an individual for whom you are caring should worsen and and perhaps greater care is required either daily or on a permanent residential basis, the situation of anyone on 'the books' of the local council social services can and should be re-assessed in order that an on-going and up-to-date record of the needs and condition of the person being cared for is on file.

For the general advice of Almoners there are three areas in which a basic knowledge in the availability of benefits to members and their dependents should be acquired. They are associated with Community Charges, Housing Benefits and Income Support. Each of these subjects could well fill a chapter on its own and the best advice which can be given in a book such as this which will be read for many years after its first publication is to approach the local authority social services department and obtain such current leaflets which deal with these three subjects individually and comprehensively.

Chapter 18:

Meals on Wheels
and The Balanced Diet

This friendly term originated shortly after World War II when such a service was set up by the Women's Royal Voluntary Service which was aided by a band of voluntary workers and it was by the standards of those day that a fledgling organization was born.

The needs of those times showed that such a service was not only needed but was one means by which many thousands of elderly people could be kept in their own homes whereas the alternative would have been to take them into permanent care in hospitals and homes simply because they could no longer prepare meals and deal with their shopping and cooking. In addition the councils into whose charge the provision of such meals eventually fell were able, by providing a balanced diet which in many cases was designed and controlled by a professional dietician, to ensure that the recipients of such meals were indeed receiving the required supply of nutriments essential for elderly people living alone. The vitamin, protein and carbohydrate contents of all meals are carefully co-ordinated and balanced to ensure that the appropriate desired daily intake is correct for healthy living. It has been noticed by the author just how much the general health of an elderly lady in her mid-eighties has improved over the past five years since she has been in receipt of such meals five days a week, after caring for herself for fifteen years.

How to organize the supply of such meals is generally very easy. A telephone call to the social services department will produce a visit by a member of the team of social workers. This visit will invariably include an overall appraisal of the home environment, the general health of the individual concerned, any obvious deformities or physical abnormalities with which the person has to cope. This will generally mean that a fuller report can be produced for the files of the social services so that any additional support which is obviously required may be offered.

Leaving these other matters on one side for the moment and returning to meals on wheels, the social worker will ascertain the weekly or monthly income of the individual and if the only income is through a government retirement pension then a daily minimum fee will be payable. This increases through a range to a person of more substantial means where the daily payment for the meal will undoubtedly be greater. The foregoing and following information is given only as a guide but its accuracy can be assured as the author has a first hand knowledge of the facilities offered by the council concerned.

The delivery of meals will commence on a given date and the person to whom the meals are being supplied will be advised that a similar delivery will be made at a certain stated time every weekday and that payment for each meal will be collected at the time. Such meals will invariably come in heat proof containers and be sealed to retain that heat during the journey through to the final consumer. At Christmas and Bank holidays local facilities will vary but it is not at all unusual for the Christmas Day meal to be given free of all charge.

There is a tendency for people in the older age group to find that the whole business of shopping, preparing and cooking food is far to great for them to undertake and therefore they move, in many cases, to the simpler means of managing with snacks of this or that which are easy to prepare and often come ready prepared. There is usually little regard paid to an overall nutritional diet or to a given intake of vitamins, nitrates, protein and carbohydrates, all of which are required to ensure that skin, bones and the natural bodily functions are performed without detriment to the person concerned. The meals on wheels system is to be highly recommended for it does those things for the person without their even being aware of it and what is more keeps them in their home environment where they are undoubtedly happier than being institutionalized, which in may cases is the only alternative. Do get as much information on this facility as you can for it is truly a lifesaver in many cases and you can be sure that at least once a day someone will knock at the door and so make certain the person concerned is alive.

Chapter 19:

The Home Help

This all-embracing term means all things to all men but let us first of all examine precisely what it does and does not cover in terms of assistance within the home. A home help is generally provided when a person who is living alone and without potential family assistance is clearly unable to accomplish those simple tasks around the home, which make the difference to staying in their own accommodation rather than being removed to a public care facility. Home helps do not engage in heavy work. Their duties are principally to carry out a little light dusting, vacuuming of carpets, shopping for food, and many will collect the retirement pension for a housebound person.

Home helps are a scarce but costly commodity and as such are placed with great care by the social services department who have to maintain an extremely budget-conscious attitude otherwise they can be accused of wasting scarce resources. For this reason the home help is usually allocated for an hour two or three times a week in which to carry out the aforementioned tasks. A signature is required each time the home help carries out her duties and from time to time the need factor is re-assessed by the supervisor of the home help section.

Clearly when a stranger comes into the home of an elderly person with a task to perform there is invariably a settling down period during which the two individuals get to know each other. For this reason, if no other, the social services try to ensure wherever possible that they allocate a home help on a permanent basis who will carry out her duties for a continuing period of time, as change amongst the elderly is not easily understood or welcomed. One facet of the home help system is that by visiting an elderly person two or three times a week the home help can quickly spot the need for medical or other care, very probably before the person being looked after realizes that they need such extra attention.

Home help assistance costs money and although it is not likely that a person living entirely on a retirement pension would be asked to pay anything for this service, clearly a person with a considerably greater income would be asked to make a donation towards the provision of such a facility. Home helps can make the difference between a life of satisfaction in one's own home and a life of institutionalized monotony and boredom to say nothing of unhappiness.

From the author's own knowledge the home help has to provide references before she is taken on to the register of the local social services to provide this service and when she has been so accepted she is usually allocated a rota of 'clients' for whom she will care. It is interesting just how close relationships can become in this environment where very frequently the life of an elderly person becomes intertwined in the daily happenings of her home help. This is a first class service which can assist, both mentally as well as physically, the daily well being of an otherwise very lonely person.

Chapter 20:

Conversions to Part of the Private Home and House Renovation Grants

It is not generally appreciated that many local authorities through the agency of their social services departments are willing to consider and, if approved make alterations of a minor nature to the private dwellings of those living within their area. Such things as providing and fixing extra handrails to staircases, widening door-frames and making adjustments to entry and exit points in order to facilitate the use of wheel chairs are amongst those things which many councils are prepared to undertake without charge to the person receiving this assistance.

There is a logic in this service which may not be immediately evident. In many cases, without this facility persons whose homes are the subject of such discussions would have to be accommodated in a nursing home or hospital which would bring to the council concerned a considerably greater and ongoing charge than the relatively smaller cost of providing the facility required to allow them to remain in their own homes. It is therefore always well worth asking the social services section of the local council for their assistance in this matter, explaining at the same time that without its being provided, the likelihood of the person whose case you are presenting being able to stay in their own abode is remote.

The 1989 Local Government and Housing Act provides for House Renovation Grants and covers both large and small alterations (called 'minor' and 'major' grants). Both schemes came into operation during 1990 and there are leaflets to be obtained from all local councils covering this new Act. There are of course financial limits to such assistance and as a general guide it can be stated that subject to the financial position of the applicant a limit of £1,000 per application is the ceiling which would apply. Should there be more than one alteration or modification required then a second or third application may be submitted, but there is an upper limit for grants of £3,000 within a three year period of time.

The purpose of such grants is to assist elderly people (classified as being over 60 years of age) to remain in their own homes. There are many headings under which such grants can be made including, in general terms, the subjects of ensuring that the home is thermally efficient, that such kitchen facilities as exist are satisfactory and that bathing and toilet facilities are adequate for the incumbent's needs. All such applications for assistance under this new scheme will only be accepted after the person making the application has satisfied the authority concerned that his or her financial standing is such as to come within the terms of the Act. It can be assumed for general purposes that anyone receiving housing benefit or income support will be eligible to apply for a minor grant.

Major grants are considered on a different basis and local councils usually provide an information package. Brother Almoner would be well advised to seek out and read such information most carefully before embarking upon an application on behalf of a member or his dependants. It must be remembered that all grants for whatever reason will be made subject to the availability of money and it is usually the custom for local councils to make an annual allotment for such work. When that money is totally used all oustanding grants will be put back for consideration within the budget allocated for such work the following year.

Chapter 21:

Visiting Opticians, Chiropodists and Hearing Consultants

An elderly person who is either totally or partially housebound will very probably find great difficulty in visiting either an optician or a chiropodist. The services of both of these professional people are of course required by many of the elderly and, by the author's own experience and investigation, it has been established that both services can be provided in the home on a fee paying basis. When either service is required it is suggested that a listing of those willing to provide either service is obtained through the local social services department or through the person's own doctor. There are frequently numbers of both types of service within a few miles of the person requiring the help albeit they have never had to call on those services before.

Chiropodists will almost certainly place this new client on their books so that a regular and on-going visiting service can be provided. Although it is quite usual for a three monthly service to be provided this can of course be varied by mutual agreement. The optician has a rather more difficult role to perform in the sense that he needs space, good lighting, special equipment and time in which to carry out the services. Elderly people frequently have a need for stronger glasses as they get older especially when their main activity consists of watching television day after day. It is very often the case that a visiting optician will discover the requirement for the removal of cataracts which will mean a referral to the patient's doctor.

The onset of deafness can of course be attributed to many things from wax in the ears to a variety of medical conditions. Where such a condition exists and is clearly becoming worse the first line of approach should be through the individual's own doctor who should make the first preliminary examination. Generally, if the scale of the problem is greater that a simple removal of wax, the attention of an ear nose and throat consultant is sought for a more detailed diagnosis of the problem which, if not thought operable, may necessitate the provision of some form of hearing aid.

Once this situation has been reached the person requiring the assistance clearly has two alternatives—either to opt for the National Health Service facility or to move to the private sector. The choice is theirs and theirs alone to make. Just remember that hearing aids bought from advertisements or home visiting consultants can be very expensive and do not always provide the excellence which they are stated to provide. An elderly person would benefit very much from having the assistance of a friend with them when considering purchasing any form of hearing aid from a visiting consultant. There have been great advances in hearing aid techniques in recent years but care is needed when selecting one.

Chapter 22:

Special Care for the Blind

Those who are blind from birth have already learned to adapt to their blindness and have very probably received instruction, assistance and guidance to assist them in living with their disability. This chapter is directed not to those who have learned to live with their total lack of sight as much as to those who for a variety of reasons have suffered from diminishing sight over a number of years and finally have arrived at the point where their ability to discern people and places becomes impossible.

Clearly much help can be obtained from the National Institute for the Blind which provides some excellent pamphlets and these are of the greatest possible assistance to brother Almoner. From these useful pieces of advice he will quickly find a variety of ways in which a needy brother or any of his dependants can be helped. Once again the local social services can and will be of use in pointing him in the right direction to obtain help within the home in addition to the various facilities available to blind people generally. It is not generally known but nevertheless true that one masonic publisher, namely Ian Allan Regalia of Addlestone in Surrey (0932 820560), can provide ritual books in braille for the blind if requested and for this service they generally do not make any charge whatsoever.

The talking book service is another benefit for the blind and such mailings to and from the blind person are made without charge by the Post Office. The Quatuor Coronati Correspondence Circle (071 405 7340) has produced ten pre-recorded tapes covering a wide variety of interesting masonic topics which can be played on a normal size cassette machine. They could well be of interest to a brother who through his disability is not able to participate in such an active way in the affairs of the lodge as was probably the case prior to his loss of sight.

At the risk of repeating a statement made earlier in this book, the social services can and will become involved in caring for such a person in their loss of sight by collecting and taking them to a day centre for contact with other people and the meals on wheels service can also be brought into play should the need for such assistance be required.

Never be afraid to contact the National Institute for the Blind. It is a most caring and well structured organisation which has many years experience of caring for people who have lost their sight either from birth or in later life. Their officials will unquestionably have come across the situation with which you are faced many times before and will give you immediate help or alternatively certainly point you in the right direction so that you know where to go to get the information you require.

Depending upon the age of the person and especially if they are living in or around the London area, there exists at Seal in Kent a school for teaching blind people how to cope with their disability and also to fit them for a useful role within society if still within working age. There are of course many such centres throughout the length and breadth of the United Kingdom as reference to the National Institute for the Blind will quickly confirm.

Amongst the many existing organisations whose purpose in life is to assist those who need help in the home, it is worth mentioning that in addition to the National Institute for the Blind, the Disabled Living Foundation has many facilities for the blind. A listing is made at the end of this book of the current telephone number of this organization.

Chapter 23:

Periods of Convalescence
for the Housebound

A not very well known facility provided by the Royal Masonic Benevolent Institution for those who are in receipt of an annuity is the opportunity to take a short holiday at one of a few designated resorts. Such facilities as exist are offered as availability determines. A welfare visitor from the RMBI can make such recommendations but there is nothing whatsoever to stop brother Almoner from applying to the RMBI directly to ask for assistance in this direction if he has a case where he believes the individual concerned would benefit from such a short break.

It is also possible, subject to availability, to apply for a break in one of the RMBI homes. Such breaks can last for as long as four weeks and application for consideration for such a short holiday should be made to the RMBI Welfare Department, 110 Main Road, Sidcup, Kent. Tel No: 081–302 6225. Such a short break can usefully be applied where a dependant who needs care and attention is preventing the person who is currently caring for them from taking a holiday themselves. In such a case an application as detailed above can usefully be considered, you may be assured that it will receive sympathetic consideration. One should never lose sight of the fact that caring for an elderly person on a permanent basis can, and frequently is, very demanding and that those who care for others also deserve sympathetic consideration as well as those for whom they are caring.

The final point to be mentioned under this heading is that a short break in a Royal Masonic Benevolent Institution Home could well be the preliminary to a permanent arrangement being considered by the dependant themselves. Moving from one's own home into a totally different environment is a major undertaking and many potential residents find this a helpful way in which to 'sample' residential life in a home without having previously made the final decision to make the move permanently.

Chapter 24:

Advising the Membership of
a Brother's Passing

The death of a brother is a landmark in the history of the lodge to which he belongs. After having been a participant for perhaps twenty or thirty years and possibly in active office for much of that time, there is now a gap that will never again be filled by that brother. The news of a brother's passing will usually reach the Secretary of the lodge before it reaches the Almoner. Depending upon the timing involved the communication of the sad news will need to be handled with some speed. If brother Secretary is about to send out a summons for a meeting he can of course incorporate the news with that communication. Therefore it can quickly be seen that timing is important and will determine the action you may need to take.

Let us consider the worst example where a brother dies in the summer months and the next meeting of the lodge is not until October which is some three months away. Clearly much can and will require to be done by telephone. Brother Almoner might find it helpful to his speedy communication with the members of his lodge if he adopts the following method used with effect by a number of Almoners. First he should decide who needs to be informed then, assuming his list reaches 25 brethren he should telephone five brethren and after informing them of the sad news he should ask each one for their assistance by telephoning a further four brethren and thereby shorten the time in communicating the news.

Before starting the communication process it will always be advisable to ascertain two facts. Firstly the date and time of the funeral and the exact location of the church or crematorium, and secondlly ensure from the immediate family whether or not they have any objection to members of lodge to which their deceased family member belonged attending the funeral and also whether flowers may be sent or whether donations to an appropriate charity are requested.

It should never be assumed that because a brother was an active participant in lodge affairs that his family necessarily shared his enthusiasm for his involvement in Freemasonry. The immediate family may have strong feelings regarding who should be present at the funeral of their loved one and whilst in the majority of cases there will be no objection, the members of the lodge attending should not automatically assume that such is the case. A polite question asked very early on in the conversation with the family will clarify this point and thereby ensure that there is no infringement of the family wishes.

Chapter 25:

The Funeral of a Member

It should be remembered that 'masonic funerals' are very much an entity of the past. The following extract from the 'Points of Procedure' booklet given with every *Book of Constitutions* states under the heading Relationship of Masonry and Religion:

(ii) that there be no active participation by Masons, as such, in any part of the burial service or cremation of a Brother and that there be no Masonic prayers, readings, or exhortations either then or at the graveside subsequent to the interment, since the final obsequies of any human being, Mason or not, are complete in themselves and do not call in the case of a Freemason for any additional ministrations. That if it is wished to recall and allude to his Masonic life and actions, this can appropriately be done at the next Lodge Meeting in the presence of his Brethren, or at a specifically arranged Memorial Service.

Whilst it will be the wish of many brethren to attend the funeral of a deceased member of the lodge, great care should be taken to ensure that the size of the party attending in no way invades the privacy of the family of the deceased member. It is sometimes the wish of the deceased brother or his spouse that a pair of white gloves are placed on the coffin. There is no ruling against such an action providing, as with all matters of a masonic nature, due decorum is shown.

Brother Almoner should always report to the lodge at its next meeting on the death of a member and the matters attendant thereto such as the funeral, those who attended, and any other material facts in order that such information can be recorded for posterity in the minutes of the lodge. It is also recommended that the service and duration of a brother's membership are similarly noted for the history of the lodge.

Chapter 26

Informing Grand Lodge, Province, District or London of the Death of a Member

Although strictly speaking it is the responsibility of brother Secretary, the communicating of the death of brother to the appropriate masonic authority is always both welcomed and appreciated in order that further distress is not caused to the bereaved family of the late member by the transmission of masonic correspondence which can so very easily occur when such information is not passed speedily and accurately to the proper authorities. To make certain that this does not happen, brother Almoner should agree with brother Secretary as to who is to pass on the information. For the sake of formality the undermentioned list will assist brother Almoner when the death of a member occurs.

Grand Officers.	Inform the Grand Secretary at Freemasons' Hall, Great Queen Street, London, WC2B 5AZ.
SLGR or LGR or SLGCR or LGCR.	Inform the London Grand Rank Association at Freemasons' Hall, Great Queen Street, London, WC2B 5TY.
Provincial or District Grand Officers.	Inform the appropriate Provincial or District Office.
Other Orders.	It is always helpful if those responsible for the administration of other masonic degrees are also informed of the death of a brother where he is known to have had membership.

NOTE: Items of masonic regalia can be a constant sad reminder of a brother's membership and are usually of little interest to the spouse or family of the brother concerned. An offer to collect and return them to their source is usually welcomed for it removes from the family the need to seek advice or information regarding their disposal. Where such an offer is made and accepted brother Almoner would be well advised to remove ALL masonic regalia albeit that perhaps some is not within his masonic experience. Subsequent enquiries made of brethren involved in other degrees will quickly elicit the correct destination to which such items should be directed.

Chapter 27:
What To Do When Someone Dies

The work entailed when someone dies usually falls into the following series of actions. First of all, on the assumption that the death occurred in a hospital where the person concerned had been resident for a given period of time:

1. The hospital will issue a certificate of death which is intended for the use of the local Registrar of Births, Deaths and Marriages whose address can be ascertained either from the hospital almoner or from the local telephone book. Where a cremation is to occur two signatures are required certifying the cause of death.

2. This certificate when received should be taken to the aforementioned Registrar who will in turn issue an order for Burial or Cremation (which is required by the undertaker before either can take place). The Registrar will also issue a Certificate of Registration of Death which may be required for Social Security and other reasons. In addition to the foregoing the Registrar will also provide certified copies of the Death Certificate which will be required by Solicitors, Banks, Insurance companies and many other similar organizations with which the deceased person may have had dealings either financial or legal. A fee will usually be charged for the provision of such documents. In some cases several copies will be required depending upon the deceased persons affairs and these days a photocopy service is provided by Registrars on the appropriate forms and paper.

The Registrar will require both Birth and Marriage Certificates as well as the Medical card of the deceased person if these are available. The Registrar will also require the date of death (where applicable) of the spouse of the deceased person.

Pension books should be returned to the local office of the Department of Health and Social Security and a receipt obtained for their delivery.

3. You may now approach the undertaker and arrange the timing and date of the funeral.

4. Communicate the details thus agreed to the brethren of the lodge.

Let us now look at the situation where a brother or his dependants die at home quite suddenly having not apparently suffered with any particular illness prior to the death. In this case the doctor of the deceased person should be contacted. He may well wish to advise the police if there are any suspicious circumstances. Presuming that this is not the case it is very likely if the doctor has not been treating the deceased person for any particular illness and had not seen him or her within the last 14 days, that he will not issue a Medical Certificate but will refer the case to the Coroner for the area in which the deceased person lived.

The purpose of such a referral is to enable a *post-mortem* to be carried out and it should be noted here that all expenses connected with such a *post-mortem* are paid for by the Coroner's office. Depending upon the outcome of the *post-mortem* the Coroner will either issue an Order for Burial or a Certificate for Cremation if the cause of death is medical or else if there is another cause such as foul play or a disease of an industrial type, the Coroner may well call for an inquest to be held. There any many variations of the issue of certificates in such cases and the Coroner's office will be pleased to advise you of the procedure to be followed whatever the cause of death. Assuming you have now received from the Coroner the necessary certificate for burial or cremation you can then proceed as detailed previously.

NOTE: It is worth mentioning here that in cases of hardship the Royal Masonic Benevolent Institution will assist with funeral expenses, subject to an investigation of the applicants financial situation.

Chapter 28

Probate—Letters of Administration— Powers of Attorney

Probate is the term given to the obtaining of a certificate which gives 'legitimacy' to a Will. It is not necessary to obtain probate where the assets are small or where the spouse is the sole beneficiary. It is necessary to obtain probate where a house is involved which is in the name of the deceased person only. It is also necessary to obtain probate where stocks and shares are held in the name of the dead person. For small sums of money many organizations are prepared to accept a properly witnessed and signed Will in which the remaining spouse is named as the sole beneficiary. Once Probate has been granted, no bank, institution or organization can continue to withhold the funds of the deceased person and they must by law then give to the person granted the Probate all that is due to the deceased person's estate.

Where large estates are concerned or where there are many beneficiaries to a Will it is always wise to obtain Probate. One person can obtain the document although if there are other family members who have a substantial share in the assets of the estate their names (up to 3) can be joined with the principal beneficiary. It really is quite surprising just how many people become disturbed at the thought of applying for Probate. The term 'being granted probate' simply means being given a certificate which proves a Will as being legal, which when granted allows the executor named to carry out the details outlined in the document for which probate has been granted. To show how simple such matters can be, let us look at two quite different cases, though this is done merely to explain the procedure, without suggesting that brother Almoner is necessarily the person on whom the duty will fall.

The first, and frequently the most usual case, is where a spouse dies and has left a Will. In such a case and where the circumstances stated above apply the remaining partner can if it is thought necessary apply for the granting of Probate. This is done by making an application through the nearest local Probate Registry, alternatively an application can be made by post to the Principal Registry, Somerset House, Strand, London, WC2R 1LP. A telephone call to 071–936 6000 requesting the requisite forms will ensure that everything required to enable you to make an application is forthcoming. With such application forms will come a scale of charges (payable at the subsequent interview) which are directly related to the size of the estate for which Probate is being sought.

Answering the questions set out in the forms is a relatively simple matter and when completed, they should be sent to the address shown, together with a copy of the Death Certificate. Within a few days a letter will be received advising the date and time for a face to face interview (usually about four weeks hence) to deal with the matter. Such an interview is informal and usually lasts only ten to twenty minutes for a simple case to perhaps half an hour for one which is rather more complicated. Providing that everything is in order and that the details are straightforward, Probate will usually be granted within two or three weeks after the interview. This interview is simply to confirm that the details submitted on the forms are correct and it should be realized that such interviews are being conducted every day in a number of local Probate Registries throughout the length and breadth of the country. Therefore the person making the application should not worry about the 'officialdom' aspect of such an interview for such interviews are friendly helpful meetings and it will be found that the applicant is quickly put at ease by the person conducting it.

This is a simple matter and need not require the involvement of a solicitor or other legal entity. The member of staff who deal with such requests are skilled at summing up speedily the requirements of a particular case and the formal granting of Probate will be carried out quite quickly after the interview has taken place. The purpose of the interview is to ascertain and confirm the facts appertaining to the deceased person's estate and the right and authority of the person applying for such Probate to do so.

When you have received the Probate you now have the full authority of the Court to carry out such matters as paying the expenses of the estate left by the deceased and other such financial affairs as may become necessary to complete the handing over of whatever estate is left to its rightful new owner. You can obtain extra copies of the Probate for (currently) 25 pence for each copy. These will be useful if you have to deal with various authorities such as Banks, Stockbrokers, Building Societies, Insurance Companies *etc.*

It would be our advice that if the estate is large and especially where such matters as capital gains or inheritance tax are being brought into play, that independent advice in the form of a solicitor be engaged to carry out the necessary paper-work, for the legislation associated with such matters is detailed and constantly changing and it is worth obtaining professional help which will undoubtedly prove well worth the fees involved. In any case, it is essential that the estate should be administered to the entire satisfaction of all the beneficiaries involved. Whoever has this responsibility would be well advised to obtain written confirmation of this from every person concerned in the settlement.

Where the deceased person has NOT left a will it will be necessary for Letters of Administration to be granted which are similar in many ways to Probate in that they attest to the fact that the person applying for them is the rightful claimant under the Laws of Intestacy. It would be our advice that such applications are best dealt with by a solicitor, although this is not a statutory requirement and if a family friend can carry out this duty then there is nothing whatsoever to prevent such an action proceeding.

Let us now move to the subject of Power(s) of Attorney. This rather severe heading means very simply that one person has given another person authority to act in their place with full legal entitlement to take such actions as the person receiving the Power of Attorney so decides. It is often the case that a Power of Attorney will have limiting factors, such as allowing the payment of funds from a designated bank account and nothing else. The size and scope of a Power of Attorney is decided by the person granting it in the first place, and it can be as limiting or as full as the person giving it so wishes.

There are basically two types of Power of Attorney. The first gives the person so named the authority to act in place of the person giving the authority and to act in his stead for the reasons given whilst that Power of Attorney exists. The second is called an Enduring Power of Attorney which is different from the former type since it does as the name implies continue after the person granting it in the first place becomes incapable for whatever reason from exercising the management of their own affairs. The Enduring Power of Attorney is frequently used where the individuals concerned are of considerable age or know that a terminal illness will at some stage in the future render them incapable or unable to manage their own affairs.

There are special forms which should be obtained for such matters (Enduring Powers of Attorney Regulations 1990 (S.I. 1376). This is a rather more complex subject than the former straightforward Power of Attorney and brother Almoner would be well counselled to seek professional help before giving any advice to the family members of a brother whose situation requires such a course of action to be considered.

Chapter 29:

Entry into an RMBI Home

A question sometimes asked by elderly members of the craft or their dependants who find the day to day problems of caring for themselves, cleaning their homes, shopping and the general physical requirements of daily life getting beyond their capability is: 'should I apply to go into an RMBI home where I will not have the worry of having to cope with all those things which are becoming more than I can manage'? The RMBI currently operates some 15 homes situated in various parts of the country where the standard of care is second to none.

Clearly there are eligibility factors for those considering this course of action and these are well stated in a leaflet especially produced for those who are thinking of making an application for admission into such a home. This leaflet which is available from the RMBI 20 Great Queen Street, London WC2B 5BG, (Tel No: 071–405 8341) gives a description of the various homes available and their precise location. In the most general of terms the RMBI will usually only admit those applicants who, providing they have satisfied the financial rules, can wash, dress and feed themselves and also walk unaided apart that is from using a walking stick where necessary.

For those who are unsure of taking such a final step it is possible for a 'short stay' to be arranged whereby an applicant can spend a few weeks in such a home to see whether or not the image they have created for themselves of 'life' in an RMBI home actually equates with the facts. Such 'breaks' can last from one to four weeks and can also be used for two other situations. This facility has been referred to briefly in Chapter 23 but it may be of assistance to brother Almoner if it is now dealt with in greater detail.

Firstly, it is possible to obtain assistance by way of a short break for a person who is being cared for in his or her own home or in that of a relative when that relative requires a short holiday but cannot leave the person for whom they are caring without available and constant help. Secondly, such short breaks can assist where a person who lives alone needs a short stay, perhaps after a severe illness or operation where they need time to recover their strength before coping with normal life once again.

In **ALL** cases an application should be made to the RMBI Welfare Department at 110 Main Road, Sidcup, Kent DA14 6NG whose telephone number is 081–302 6225. This department will issue the necessary forms for completion. There are some fundamental questions which will require to be answered which can briefly be summarised as follows:

Name and Address of the Applicant.

Name and Number of the Lodge.

Name and Address of the Lodge Almoner.

Details of the brother's Initiation date.

Years in which he has subscribed to the Craft.

His present masonic rank.

Details of his present financial situation.

Confirmation that the applicant is ambulant, and can wash, dress and feed himself.

There can be little doubt that life in an RMBI home will be different from that which the person so applying has enjoyed previously for the simple reason that there are rules by which the home has to be run. There are, for example, such simple things such as the timing of meals, advising the Matron or her Deputy if one is going out and does not expect to return until late in the evening and the acceptance that one can only have a certain very limited range of one's personal possessions in one's room. These have to be thought about carefully before a commitment is made. A person who cannot accept such limitations on their freedom is clearly not going to be happy as a resident in an RMBI home. It is essential therefore that brother Almoner mentions such facts when he counsels anyone considering such a permanent move in their later years

Let us assume for a moment that brother Almoner has arrived at the point where such facts have been mentioned and have been accepted and the applicant wishes to proceed. What then happens? A form as described previously should be obtained from the Welfare Department, duly completed, and returned as soon as possible. On receipt of the form a Welfare Visitor (all of whom are qualified nurses) will then call upon the applicant by appointment to discuss the application and to ask for confirmation of certain points relevant to the consideration of such an admission.

Do remember that there will certainly be a waiting period before a new applicant can be admitted to one of the more frequently sought homes around the London area in particular and clearly many applicants have to wait until a vacancy arises before an offer to appear for an interview is granted. What happens from this point onwards is very much in the hands of the Welfare Department which may be contacted if advice of the ongoing situation regarding a particular application is sought.

Finally and most importantly it must be remembered that anyone being admitted to an **RMBI** home even though they are paying towards their care will, without question, be receiving a high proportion of the cost of caring for them from the donations of the members of the Craft who subscribe to the **RMBI** Every resident without exception is financially supported in this way. It is therefore the duty of the Welfare Department to ensure that 'need' is the first consideration and those who are financially able to provide such 'need' for themselves will not be high on the list of those seeking admission and indeed may not qualify at all.

Chapter 30:

The Masonic Trust for Girls and Boys

A situation may occasionally arise where a member either dies or is unable to support his family for a whole range of reasons. This is where the help, guidance and assistance of the Masonic Trust for Girls and Boys will come to the aid of brother Almoner. Let us look as the explanation given for the existence of the Trust as outlined in the Masonic Year Book:

'The objects of the Trust are to relieve poverty and to advance education. Those eligible for assistance are the children (including adopted children, step-children and children of the family) of any age, of Freemasons under the United Grand Lodge of England, who are considered to be in need of such assistance. The aim is to provide, so far as possible, the same opportunities in life as would have been available to the child concerned had death or misfortune not occurred within the family. The Trust also has power, provided that sufficient funds are available, to grant assistance to any child who is not the child of a Freemason.

The range of facilities available to assist the children of those members of the Craft who for whatever reason find themselves either unable to support or educate their own children is considerable. The forms of aid range from education at the school for girls at Rickmansworth in Hertfordshire, which caters for residential as well as day pupils, to arranging education at a school nearer to the home of the family. These are but two of the many options which can be considered and arranged.

For those boys who are either already undertaking an apprenticeship to those who wish to do so, the Masonic Boys Welfare Fund is able to support a boy during the period covered by that apprenticeship albeit that this could take seven years. There are also funds available for the purchase of books and equipment where the total family income is very low. There are also several special funds ranging from an educational trust to travelling scholarships in various parts of the world.

Brother Almoner should obtain from this well known organization a list of its facilities in order that, should such a situation arise concerning the children of a brother in need or one who has died at an early age and left a young family who require educating, he will not be found wanting when asked 'what can be done to help'?

Almoners whose lodges are in Provinces and Districts are advised, as their first step, to seek assistance from their respective Provincial or District Grand Secretary who will supply the necessary forms for completion and advise through the Provincial or District Almoner the best way of progressing any application for help.

There are various other funds in existence covering a wide range of availabilities, all of which are administered by the MTGB. They cover a wide area from the Fund providing Travelling Scholarships (2), the Ruspini Fund, the Burwood Fund and two other bursaries, the qualifying details of which can all be explored when a suitable case comes before brother Almoner. The details and qualifications of each fund are available on request from the MTGB. You can be quite certain that any child can and will be helped for the funds of the MTGB are large and grow annually. Members of the Craft subscribe large amounts of money for assisting such needy cases and brother Almoner should not hesitate to seek assistance where a genuine need exists.

The Masonic Trust for Girls and Boys can be contacted on 071–405 2644.

Chapter 31:

Funding the Role Effectively

Experience has shown that a large number of lodge Almoners tend to finance the calls upon their time and travelling themselves rather than give a 'bill' to brother Treasurer, regarding such a form of remittance as 'foreign' to their understanding of the role. Nothing can be further from the truth. The job of Almoner, for a job it most certainly is, falls into the same category as that provided by brother Secretary and no one expects him to pay for the mailing of the summons and other clerical matters do they?

The role of Almoner is in large part performed outside the lodge itself and such travelling expenses as are incurred together with telephone calls and postage should be properly accounted for and a detailed expense sheet submitted to brother Treasurer at an appropriate time. It must be remembered that although perhaps one Almoner may well be financially capable and not worry about the costs he has to pay out, he may well be followed by an equally diligent Almoner who is perhaps living entirely on a state pension and cannot therefore afford the luxury of assisting the lodge by paying all the costs he incurs.

In any well run lodge brother Treasurer should have a budget for the anticipated expenses for the following year; such things as will be included are fees to Grand Lodge as well as those to Provincial or District Grand Lodge and the associated costs of running the various meetings throughout the year together with the cost of producing the summons for each meeting and its subsequent despatch to the members.

There is a very good case for brother Treasurer to discuss with brother Almoner an amount of money which it would be as well to 'reserve' against the eventuality of the Almoner's services being needed and monies requiring to be spent. If brother Almoner carries out his duties as explained in this book, an amount of £100 would not be regarded as too large and in the event that the occasion does not arise and the money is not needed, nothing is lost in the overall scheme of things is it?

The role of the Almoner is to 'dispense' charity in whatever form it is appropriate from visiting the sick to remembering the dependants of those who are no longer alive. Freemasonry quite correctly presents itself as a caring organization and it is therefore quite wrong for brother Almoner to attempt to 'fund' the cost of carrying out his own duties, for such costs are the responsibility of the whole lodge not just of one officer.

Chapter 32:

New Masonic Samaritan Fund

Set up in November 1990, this fund was established to provide for the relief of poverty and sickness for the ill and infirm amongst Freemasons, their wives, children and dependants.

The reason for the word 'New' in front of the well known Samaritan Fund of the Royal Masonic Hospital is to differentiate between the two different organizations. It is hoped that eventually the two schemes which currently run side by side will find a means by which they can combine their worthy efforts. Until that time arrives they will continue to operate under separate management teams.

The choice of the word 'Samaritan' is of course immediately understandable and recognizable to all members of the Craft and such requests as may come the way of brother Almoner for help with medical and other expenses should be directed to this new organization as it will assist where the applicant concerned falls within its rules for assistance.

The telephone number to which such enquiries should be referred to is 071–405 1550.

Chapter 33:

Administration

Having now very nearly reached the end of this book the reader will realize that there is considerably more to the role of the lodge Almoner than is perhaps at first imagined. What this book has endeavoured to do is not to try to make the reader an expert on every kind of approach he might receive during his tenure of office but rather to give him the direction in which he should look to become better informed about a given situation. Help is all around us but frequently we do not know where to start to look for it. It is hoped that by reference to this book the lodge Almoner will find a starting point from which he can increase his knowledge.

In the enthusiasm which frequently accompanies the challenge to 'sort out a situation' it can sometimes be the case that the accurate recording of the events which preceded the call for help are not noted with all their relevant details. It is essential for brother Almoner to make accurate 'case notes' from the moment he first meets the relatives or dependants of a member. He will need for example the full names of the member, the date of his initiation, the length of his membership of the Craft and of the lodge as well as his final rank in the Craft.

The details of his family, children and ages, current schooling arrangements, financial and educational commitments, mortgage repayments where appropriate, and such other relevant details as may be applicable to the issue at hand. The forms sent by the various Institutions and the Grand Charity will certainly require a comprehensive account of the circumstances in which assistance is being sought as well as details of the individuals involved and it is a wise Almoner who already has most of this information on file for he can then dispense with the necessity of going over the same ground again with those he is trying to help.

Ensure that copies are kept of all forms completed so that if reference has to be made to them in the years which follow, an accurate 'pen portrait' can be established regarding the circumstances which appertained at the beginning. It is also good advice to maintain a 'running' series of notes at the front of each file, showing each and every stage connected with the particular case so that the progress of events as they unfolded can be 'seen at a glance' and thus future steps can be discussed and decisions made with the benefit of a complete and accurate set of records.

Remember that some 'cases' can continue for 15 or 20 years, particularly where a very young family is involved and especially if the educational concerns encountered involve supporting a young child from its junior school through to the completion of its education at university. It could well be that where such a long-running case is involved that the brother Almoner referring to the notes made 20 years ago may well be three or four Almoners removed from the brother who was originally involved with their completion. So the message is clear, think ahead to the days when you are no longer the Almoner and remember that the work of 'caring' for the membership and their dependants continues even after we stand down from office.

Chapter 34:

Useful Addresses and Telephone Numbers

THE UNITED GRAND LODGE OF ENGLAND
Freemasons' Hall,
Great Queen Street,
LONDON WC2B 5AZ.   071–831 9811

LONDON GRAND RANK ASSOCIATION
PO Box 324,
60 Great Queen Street,
LONDON WC2B 5TY.   071–405 1671

THE ROYAL MASONIC HOSPITAL
Ravenscourt Park,
LONDON W6 0TN.   071–748 4611

ROYAL MASONIC BENEVOLENT INSTITUTION
20, Great Queen Street,
LONDON WC2B 5BG.   071–405 8341

ROYAL MASONIC BENEVOLENT INSTITUTION,
Welfare Department,
110, Main Road,
SIDCUP,
Kent DA14 6NG.   081–302 6225

MASONIC TRUST FOR GIRLS AND BOYS
31, Great Queen Street,
LONDON WC2B 5AG.   071–405 2644

GRAND CHARITY
Freemasons' Hall,
60, Great Queen Street,
LONDON WC2B 5AZ.   071–831 9811

NEW MASONIC SAMARITAN FUND
26, Great Queen Street
LONDON WC2B 5BB.   071–404 1550

QCCC LTD,
Freemasons' Hall,
60, Great Queen Street,
LONDON WC2B 5BA.   071–405 7340

ROYAL MASONIC BENEVOLENT INSTITUTION HOMES

HARWOOD COURT—HOVE, SUSSEX	0273 739515
DEVONSHIRE COURT—OADBY, LEICS	0533 714171
SCARBOROUGH COURT—CRAMLINGTON, NORTHUMBERLAND	0670 712215
PRINCE GEORGE DUKE OF KENT COURT —CHISLEHURST, KENT	081–467 0081
CONNAUGHT COURT—FULFORD, YORK	0904 626238
LORD HARRIS COURT—SINDLESHAM, BERKSHIRE	0734 787496
PRINCE OF WALES COURT—PORTHCAWL, GLAMORGAN	0656 715311
QUEEN ELIZABETH COURT—LLANDUDNO	0492 77276
JAMES TERRY COURT—CROYDON, SURREY	081–688 1745
CORNWALLIS COURT—BURY ST EDMUNDS	0284 68028
ZETLAND COURT—WESTBOURNE, BOURNEMOUTH	0202 739169
CADOGAN COURT—EXETER, DEVON	0392 51436
*ECCLESHOLME—ECCLES, MANCHESTER	061 7889517
*THE TITHEBARN–GREAT CROSBY, LIVERPOOL	051 9243683
*FAIRLAWN—ST ANNES, LANCS	0253 736110

*HANNAY MASONIC RESIDENTIAL HOMES

OUTSIDE CHARITIES AND ASSOCIATIONS

AGE CONCERN	081-640 5431
ASSOCIATION FOR SPINA BIFIDA & HYDROCEPHALUS	071-388 1382
ASSOCIATION OF RETIRED PERSONS	071-828 0500
BRITISH DIABETIC ASSOCIATION	071-323 1531
BRITISH EPILEPSY ASSOCIATION	0345 023153
BRITISH HEART FOUNDATION	071-935 0185
CEREBAL PALSY HELPLINE	0800 626216
CHARTERED ACCOUNTANTS BENEVOLENT ASSOCIATION	071-588 2662
CINEMA AND TELEVISION BENEVOLENT FUND	071-437 6567
CITIZENS ADVICE BUREAU	SEE LOCAL DIRECTORY
COMMONWEALTH SOCIETY FOR THE DEAF	071-631 5311
CONFECTIONERS BENEVOLENT FUND	071-629 7107
CRUSE—CARE FOR THE BEREAVED	081-940 4818
CYSTIC FIBROSIS RESEARCH TRUST	081-464 7211
DISABLED LIVING FOUNDATION	071-289 6111
DSS—FREE TELEPHONE HELP LINE	0800 666 555
ECZEMA NATIONAL SOCIETY	071-388 4097
FURNISHING TRADES BENEVOLENT ASSOCIATION	071-836 6082
HELP THE AGED	071-253 0253
MENTAL HEALTH FOUNDATION	071-580 0145
MUSICIANS BENEVOLENT FUND	071-636 4481
NATIONAL ASSOCIATION OF WIDOWS	021-643 8348
PSORIASIS ASSOCIATION	0604 711129
ROYAL BRITISH LEGION	071-930 8131
ROYAL AIR FORCE BENEVOLENT FUND	071-580 8343
ROYAL AIR FORCE DEPENDANTS FUND	071-580 4306
ROYAL ASSOCIATION FOR DISABILITY & REHABILITATION	071-637 5400
ROYAL NATIONAL INSTITUTE FOR THE BLIND	0345 023153
ROYAL NATIONAL INSTITUTE FOR THE DEAF	071-387 8033

SOLDIERS, SAILORS AND AIR FORCE ASSOCIATION	071–222 9221
ST DUNSTAN'S FOR SERVICE WAR BLINDED	071–723 5021
THE SPASTICS SOCIETY	0800 62616

It is not suggested that this list is comprehensive. The details of those organizations listed are shown in order to give the reader an example of the wide range of help that exists should it be needed. Almoners are strongly counselled to investigate every possible avenue which may be related directly or indirectly with the person for whom he may be seeking assistance either from a previous profession or working environment or an illness related need.

Chapter 35:

General

One facet of the 'help' available which has not been discussed in this book is the existence of the hundreds if not thousands of trade associations many of which have substantial funds secured over many years for the sole function of assisting members and past members (and in many cases their relatives) of those trades or association who have a call upon such funds as a matter of right.

Brother Almoner should remember that when the subject of assistance in any of its forms is raised for whatever reason he needs to include in his discussion with the person (or spouse of the person) questions relating to their previous trade or profession for it might just be that an extra form of assistance from this source is available. Remember also that the various Trade Unions have similar funds upon which members and past members have a call. Frequently such avenues of approach are not used and this can be to the detriment of the person requiring the help.

Remember also that those who have served with the armed forces, particularly in a full time capacity can call upon the facilities of the Soldiers, Sailors and Air Force Association as well as those of the Royal British Legion who assist in the maintenance of many past members of the armed forces in their closing years. It is often the case that with a little diligence and persistence, help can be forthcoming or be made available from two or three sources and not entirely from those of a masonic nature.

We live today in a society which cares more for the sick and needy than ever before. The government provides basic relief through legislation to a given standard and local councils are required to provide by statute various forms of individual home care for the sick and disabled. Organizations such as those already mentioned can also make available extra funds to support such needs so that it can immediately be seen that 'dumping' the entire problem of any particular case on to the relevant masonic authority is frequently not the complete answer to the problem. A well produced portfolio covering such questions as may be relevant would benefit any Almoner who wishes to be on top of his office and furthermore it negates the requirement to build such a list of questions each time a new 'case' arises.

Finally and as the last paragraph in this book may we remind every brother Almoner that 'help' is all around him and if approached correctly that help will willingly be given. Never be afraid to ask if help in any form can be given from any organization for you will be surprised just how often you will receive an affirmative reply.